Ada's Violin

The Story of the
Recycled Orchestra of Paraguay

SUSAN HOOD

Illustrated by
SALLY WERN COMPORT

SIMON & SCHUSTER BOOKS FOR YOUNG READERS

NEW YORK   LONDON   TORONTO   SYDNEY   NEW DELHI

"For me, the violin means everything . . . life."
—Ada Ríos

For Favio, Cola, Ada, and all the children of the Recycled Orchestra . . . Play on!
—S. H.

For Favio Chávez, the Recycled Orchestra, and the dedicated teachers
who inspire a spark and ignite the world

—S. W. C.

SIMON & SCHUSTER BOOKS FOR YOUNG READERS
An imprint of Simon & Schuster Children's Publishing Division
1230 Avenue of the Americas, New York, New York 10020
Text copyright © 2016 by Susan Hood
Illustrations copyright © 2016 by Sally Wern Comport
For information about special discounts for bulk purchases, please contact
Simon & Schuster Special Sales at 1-866-506-1949 or business@simonandschuster.com.
The Simon & Schuster Speakers Bureau can bring authors to your live event.
For more information or to book an event, contact the Simon & Schuster Speakers Bureau
at 1-866-248-3049 or visit our website at www.simonspeakers.com.
Book design by Laurent Linn
The text for this book is set in ITC Legacy Sans Std.
The illustrations for this book were created from a hybrid technique of collage,
acrylic glazes and paints, drawings, and digital mediums, then executed on stipple paper.
Manufactured in China
1116 SCP
4 6 8 10 9 7 5 3
Library of Congress Cataloging-in-Publication Data
Hood, Susan, 1954– author.
Ada's violin : the story of the Recycled Orchestra of Paraguay / Susan Hood ;
illustrated by Sally Wern Comport.
pages cm
ISBN 978-1-4814-3095-1 (hardcover : alk. paper) — ISBN 978-1-4814-3096-8 (eBook)
1. Bordados, Ada Maribel Rios—Juvenile literature. 2. Orquesta de Instrumentos Reciclados Cateura—
Juvenile literature. 3. Orchestra—Paraguay—Asunción—Juvenile literature.
4. Orchestral musicians—Paraguay—Asunción—Juvenile literature.
I. Comport, Sally Wern, illustrator. II. Title.
ML3930.B63H66 2016
784.206'0892121—dc23
2015004299

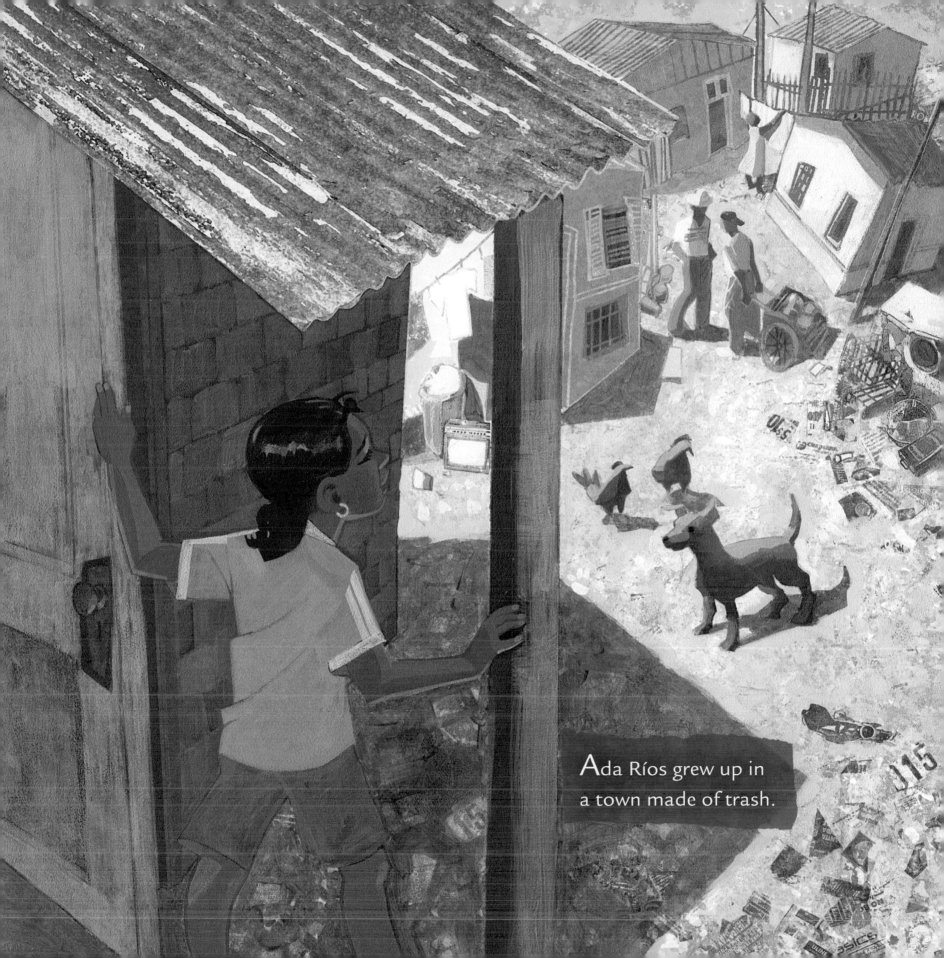

Ada Ríos grew up in a town made of trash.

Every morning at dawn, Ada heard the first garbage trucks rumble and roll down the road to Cateura. *Beep, beep, beep!* Backing into the landfill, they tipped their loads up and up and—*CRASH!* The trash came tumbling down—fifteen hundred tons each day.

Ada and her friends watched as the *gancheros*
(recyclers) scrambled, tearing into plastic bags
with long-handled hooks, pushing aside moldy
produce, and grabbing anything they could recycle
or sell. The going rates? "Five cents for a pound of
cardboard, ten cents for a pound of plastic."

This noisy, stinking, sweltering slum was not the most nurturing neighborhood. Ada watched, eyes wide, but she didn't say much.

And yet she liked to imagine each garbage truck was "a box of surprises." One never knew what might be inside. Her father had found appliances, toys, perfumes, and antique watches. One woman even discovered a small box full of gold jewelry!

Little did Ada know, there was a bigger surprise waiting for her in the landfill.

Every day when Ada's parents went to work, Grandmother Mirian cared for Ada and her little sister, Noélia. Grandma loved to sing rock 'n' roll songs from the 1960s. The girls grew up to the tunes of the Beatles, Simon and Garfunkel, and Creedence Clearwater Revival. Ada loved to sing too (but only when no one was listening).

Ada's dad brightened the night with stories and songs of great musicians. He turned up the radio and pointed out the sounds each instrument made. Ada heard one above all others. *Zing* went the strings of the violin!

When the girls started school, Grandma returned to work as a recycler, collecting bottles and cans in the city.

Classes let out at noon. Young Ada was in charge of Noélia until her parents were done with work.

At first the girls stayed close to home, playing with Grandma Mirian's doggies and making sand cakes in the dirt.

Soon they joined their cousins, playing hide-and-seek or a game of handball in the streets.

In time they ventured farther afield,
walking down to the bodega to get candy.

But Ada noticed the teenagers hanging out in the alleys, grumbling about life in the landfill looming ahead. What would happen to them . . . to her . . . to her little sister? She watched as the older kids turned to gangs and got into fights.

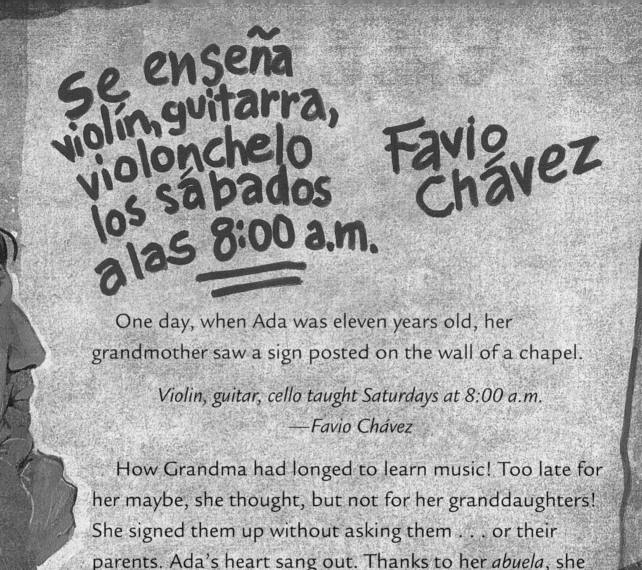

Se enseña violín, guitarra, violonchelo los sábados a las 8:00 a.m.

Favio Chávez

One day, when Ada was eleven years old, her grandmother saw a sign posted on the wall of a chapel.

Violin, guitar, cello taught Saturdays at 8:00 a.m.
—Favio Chávez

How Grandma had longed to learn music! Too late for her maybe, she thought, but not for her granddaughters! She signed them up without asking them . . . or their parents. Ada's heart sang out. Thanks to her *abuela*, she could leave her worries behind and learn to play!

At the first class the teacher, Favio Chávez, had three guitars and two violins to share. Ada chose a violin right away. But ten children had signed up. Frustrated, Ada and her friends found that there were not enough instruments to go around.

And there was a bigger problem. Everyone quickly realized that the children would need to practice at home. But it wasn't safe to be seen with an expensive instrument in Cateura, where a violin is worth more than a house.

Watching the children play amid broken glass and rusty metal, Señor Chávez knew he had to do something! He remembered a band called Les Luthiers that made its own instruments. That was it! He asked Nicolás "Cola" Gómez, a *ganchero* and carpenter, for help.

Señor Gómez found a discarded drum with a big hole in it. What could he use to fix it? He picked through the trash and discovered an old X-ray film. Would that work?

It did!

Señor Gómez kept experimenting and others, like Tito Romero, helped. Inventing instruments wasn't easy. But they fiddled around, discovering which materials hit just the right notes. They transformed oil drums into cellos, water pipes into flutes, and packing crates into guitars!

Soon there were enough instruments for all the children who wanted to play!

Ada chose a violin made from an old paint can, an aluminum baking tray, a fork, and pieces of wooden crates. Worthless to thieves, it was invaluable to her. It was a violin of her very own!

Señor Chávez set up a strict schedule of three-hour lessons. The class had no classroom so they played outside, despite the 100-degree heat and sudden downpours.

At first Ada and the others struggled. Sharps and flats clanged and clashed. "Playing an instrument is a process. It doesn't matter if one is rich or poor, ugly, fat, thin—you cannot learn to play an instrument overnight," Señor Chávez told the children.

Some kids decided it was too much work and gave up, but not Ada. After lessons she would practice at home, sometimes two hours a day.

In time the screeches, twangs, and tweets hit all the right notes. Their class became "a small island" where Chávez taught them to respect themselves and one another.

"Be kind, always say please and thank you, say you're sorry, be dedicated when you commit to something," Señor Chávez told the children.

Soon the ragtag crew of kids learned to tune in, to listen to one another, to band together. The Recycled Orchestra was born!

From then on, there was something new in the air in Cateura. *Gancheros* trudging home from the landfill might lift their heads to hear the sounds of Ada's violin . . . or the strains of Bebi's cello . . . or the strum of Noélia's guitar. A symphony of sound helped to lift them beyond the heat, the stench, and their aching backs.

With her violin, Ada could close her eyes and imagine a different life.
She could soar on the high, bright, bittersweet notes to a place far away.
She could be who she was meant to be.

As Ada's skill grew, so did her confidence. Once timid, she now took center stage playing solos. She helped teach the younger children too.

Her teachers and fellow students took note. When she was twelve years old, Ada was named a first violinist. Imagine! She was first at something!

Shortly after, she and her thirty-nine fellow musicians were invited to perform concerts in Cateura, and later in the nearby capital city of Asunción.

Word of this extraordinary orchestra spread. Soon they were asked to perform in other cities . . . and even other countries!

Ada and her friends flew on their first airplane, stayed in their first hotel, swam in the bright blue waters of Rio de Janeiro, sampled their first pastries and pineapple, and saw sights they never imagined. The world dazzled them . . . just as they dazzled the world!

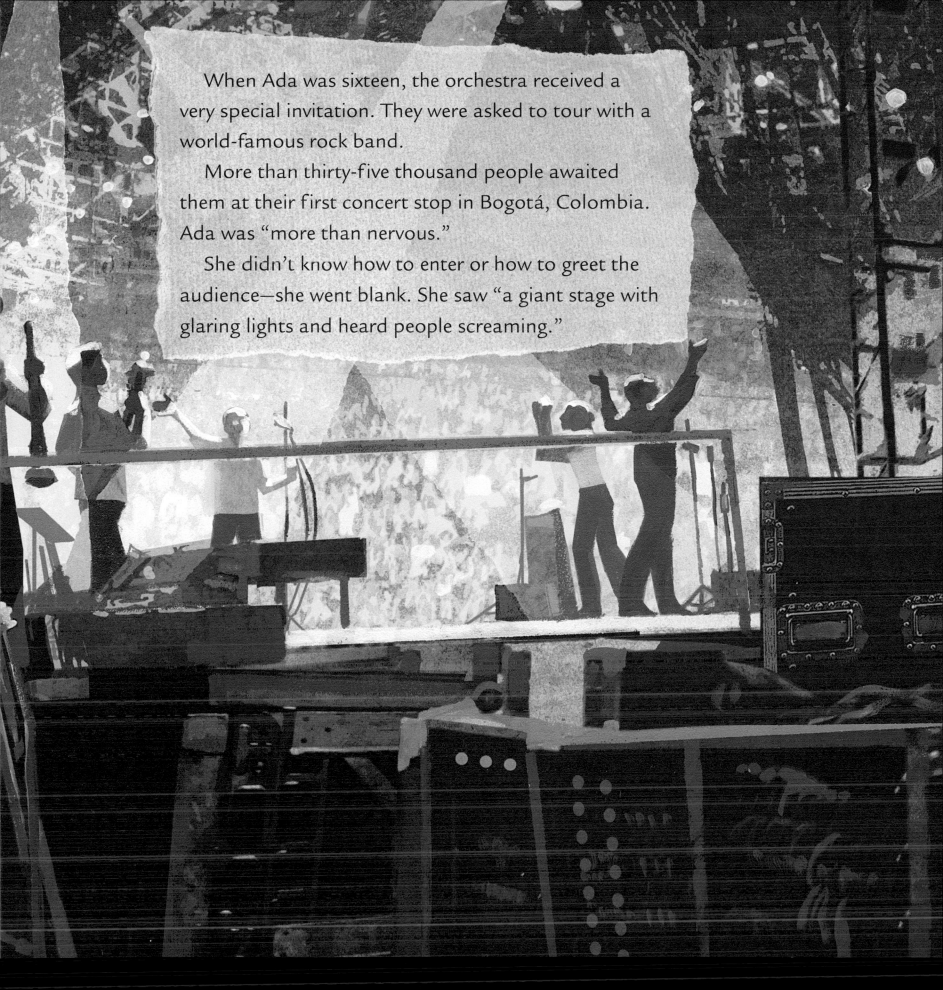

When Ada was sixteen, the orchestra received a very special invitation. They were asked to tour with a world-famous rock band.

More than thirty-five thousand people awaited them at their first concert stop in Bogotá, Colombia. Ada was "more than nervous."

She didn't know how to enter or how to greet the audience—she went blank. She saw "a giant stage with glaring lights and heard people screaming."

But she didn't have to worry.
As the Recycled Orchestra took the stage, the people who had paid to see the rock band cheered for them.

EURA! EURA! EURA!
ATeURa!
ATe

The enormous audience sang and swayed to the music as the orchestra played. And as their performance came to a close . . .

a crescendo of cheers, chants, and applause resounded across the park. The astonished kids bowed, grinning at one another. They had discovered the surprise waiting in the landfill. Buried in the trash was music.

And buried in themselves was something to be proud of.

"The world sends us garbage. We send back music."—Favio Chávez

Ada Ríos's town, Cateura, is the main garbage dump for the capital city of Asunción, Paraguay. It is one of the poorest slums in all of South America. More than twenty-five hundred families—twenty thousand people—live there on less than two dollars a day. They endure fourteen-hour days picking through the trash in the landfill to find things they can recycle and sell. Officially, children aren't allowed to work in the landfill, but that doesn't stop them. Some of the families need their help. "Whoever can carry something can work," said Ada.

Generations of Ada's family worked the landfill, including her father and grandmother. But her father later got a better job sewing and embroidering clothes. Her mom worked as a caregiver for an elderly relative. Ada and Noélia could attend school, but as children, there were still long hours with nothing to do and trouble waiting in the wings. Then a newcomer came to town.

Favio Chávez was an environmental engineer, sent to Cateura to teach safety practices to the *gancheros* working amid dangerous heaps of refuse. Laboring alongside them in the landfill, he befriended the recyclers and worried about their children. A musician himself, he decided to offer music lessons to keep the kids out of trouble. In time Chávez's music class became an orchestra, aptly named the Recycled Orchestra!

Concert invitations followed, but there were difficult roadblocks. Chávez discovered that the children didn't have the identity papers, or even birth certificates, required for travel. "They had, legally, not been born." Chávez changed all that. Today, Ada and her friends have performed concerts all over the world—in Argentina, Brazil, Canada, Colombia, England, Germany, Japan, Mexico, Norway, Palestine, Spain, the United States, and more. They have toured with the rock band Metallica and played for world dignitaries, including Pope Francis!

Money from the orchestra's concerts goes back to Cateura to help families rebuild their homes, their music school, and their lives. "Not too long ago we purchased a piece of land where we will build houses for fifteen orchestra families," said Chávez. "Ada has a new house there." This land is out of the flood zone. These families will never again have to face the evacuations that displace Cateura villagers every year when the river rises.

What started as music class for ten kids has swelled to orchestral rehearsals for two hundred students, with more than twenty-five instructors. Chávez quit his ecology job to work with the orchestra full-time. Now plans are afoot to use the Recycled Orchestra's experiences as a model to help other children living on landfills around the world.

—SUSAN HOOD

> "Music allowed us to connect with other people.
> Without even speaking the language, we understand each other."—Favio Chávez

FOR MORE INFORMATION

WEBSITES

Orquesta de Reciclados de Cateura: recycledorchestracateura.com

Landfill Harmonic: landfillharmonicmovie.com
   Information about the documentary movie produced by Alejandra Amarilla, Juliana Penaranda-Loftus, Rodolfo Madero, and Belle Murphy.

The Recycled Orchestra Exhibit at the Musical Instrument Museum: mim.org
   Eight recycled instruments from Paraguay are on permanent exhibit at this museum in Phoenix, Arizona.

VIDEOS

The Recyclers: From Trash Comes Triumph: cbsnews.com
   A segment on *60 Minutes* about the Recycled Orchestra.

YouTube.com
   La orquesta de Instrumentos Reciclados se instaló en Bogotá, Colombia
      The orchestra backstage and onstage at the opening of their concert tour with the band Metallica.

   The Recycled Orchestra of Cateura. "Nothing Else Matters" at the Metallica Tour (Chile)
      A video of the orchestra playing with Metallica.

YouTube.com (continued)

Una orquesta que convierte la basura en música
An excellent clip showcasing Favio (far right), Ada (center), and Ada's aunt Maria (left) playing with the orchestra.

"A mi manera" interpretado por la orquesta de Cateura
Ada onstage, performing "My Way," accompanied by Favio Chávez.

~ SOURCES ~

Quotations are from interviews I conducted with Ada Ríos and Favio Chávez. *Muchas gracias* to them and to Thomas Lecourt for answering my questions and to Shelley McConnell for her expert translations.

Special thanks to my editor, Christian Trimmer; my agent, Brenda Bowen; *60 Minutes* producer Michael Gavshon; and *60 Minutes* correspondent Bob Simon.

"Five cents for a pound of cardboard. Ten cents for a pound of plastic."
Simon, Bob, correspondent. Gavshon, Michael, prod. "The Recyclers: From Trash Comes Triumph." *60 Minutes*. New York: CBS, November 17, 2013, and May 18, 2014. Television show.

Note: These prices and amounts were translated and converted. In Paraguay, people use *guaraníes* (the Paraguayan coins) and kilograms, not cents or pounds. For current rates, see: xe.com/currencyconverter.

"Never doubt that a small group of thoughtful, committed citizens can change the world; indeed, it's the only thing that ever has."—Margaret Mead

In honor of this book's publication, Simon & Schuster, Inc., is making a donation to Orquesta de Instrumentos Reciclados de Cateura. To find out how you can help, e-mail orquestareciclados@gmail.com.